EX LIBRIS

Drawing stuff

YOUR NAME

ART

UP, UP, UP AND AWAY

DOODLES

Just ADD
Genius
With No
Jiggery-Pokery

SALARIYA

© The Salariya Book Company Ltd MMXI
All rights reserved. No part of this publication
may be reproduced, stored in or introduced into
a retrieval system or transmitted in any form,
or by any means (electronic, mechanical,
photocopying, recording or otherwise) without
the written permission of the publisher. Any
person who does any unauthorised act in
relation to this publication may be liable to
criminal prosecution and civil claims for
damages.

1 3 5 7 9 8 6 4 2

Visit our website at **www.book-house.co.uk**
or go to **www.salariya.com** for **free**
electronic versions of:
**You Wouldn't Want to be an Egyptian
Mummy!**
**You Wouldn't Want to be a Roman
Gladiator!**
You Wouldn't Want to be a Polar Explorer!
**You Wouldn't Want to Sail on a 19th-
Century Whaling Ship!**

A CIP catalogue record for this book is
available from the British Library.

Printed and bound in China.
Printed on paper from
sustainable sources.

Published in Great Britain in MMXI
by
Book House, an imprint of
The Salariya Book Company Ltd
25 Marlborough Place,
Brighton BN1 1UB
www.salariya.com
www.book-house.co.uk

ISBN-13: 978-1-907184-86-4

Q: What do you call a
flying skunk?
A: A smellicopter!

PROF. Zacharias Zog's

DOODLES

DOT-TO-DOT

PUZZLES!

MAZES

ART

DAFT STUFF

STUFF

SPOT THE DIFFERENCE

Splat-a -Fact™

Flight Activity Book

by

Prof. Zacharias Zog

and

Prof. Your name

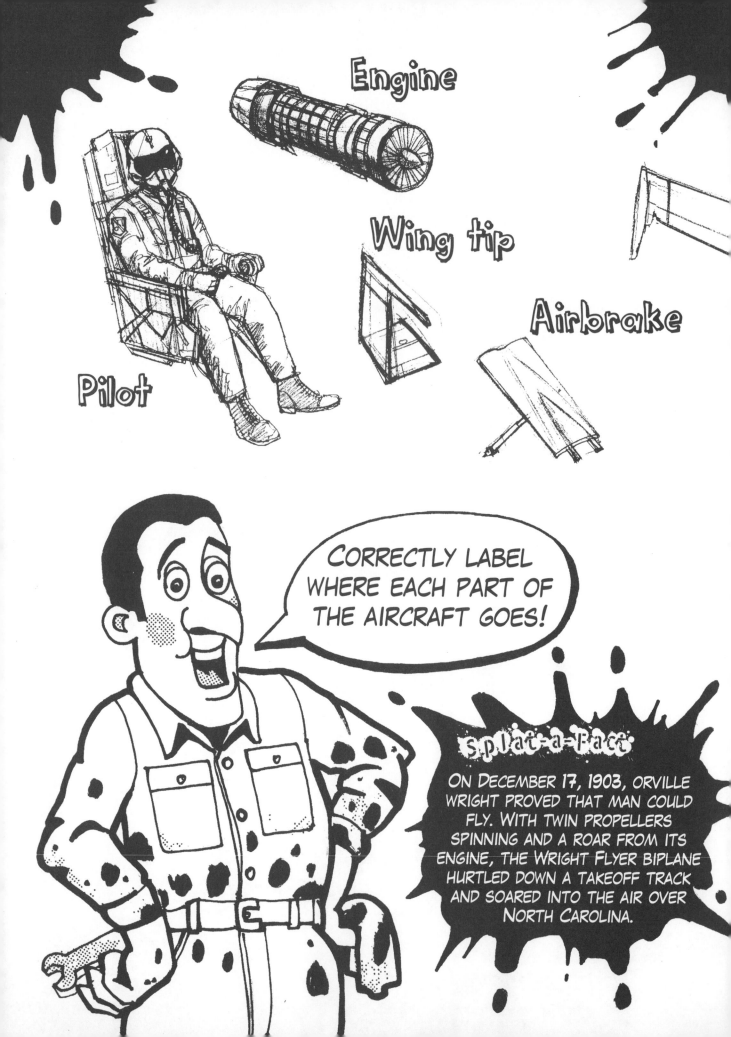

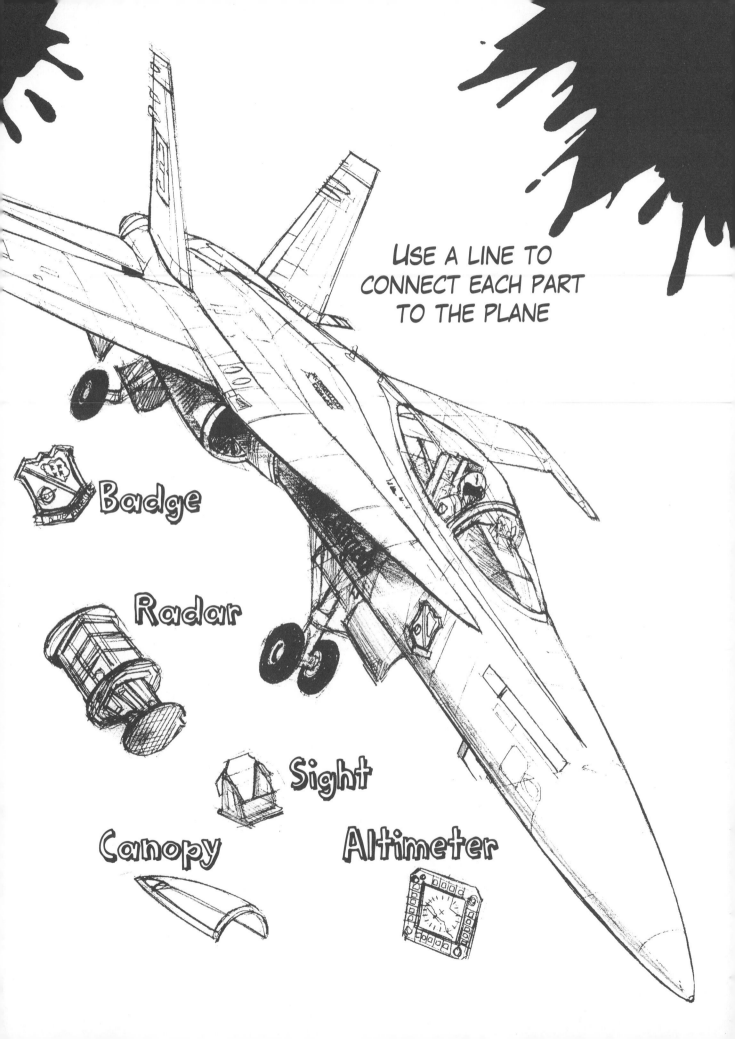

USE A LINE TO CONNECT EACH PART TO THE PLANE

Badge

Radar

Sight

Canopy

Altimeter

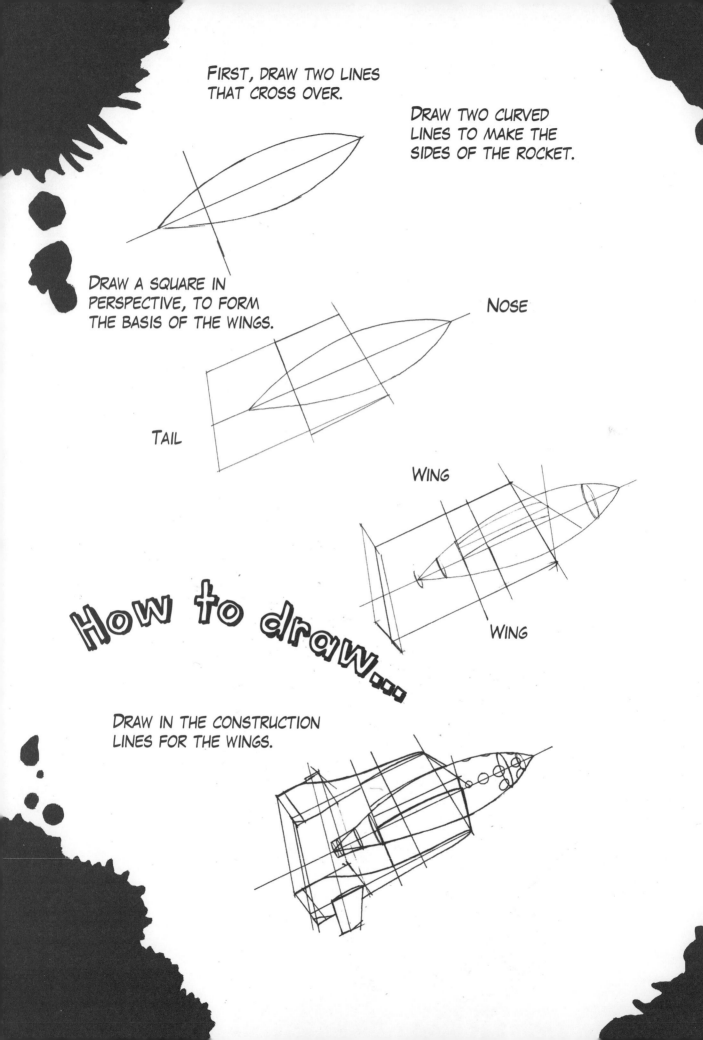

FIRST, DRAW TWO LINES THAT CROSS OVER.

DRAW TWO CURVED LINES TO MAKE THE SIDES OF THE ROCKET.

DRAW A SQUARE IN PERSPECTIVE, TO FORM THE BASIS OF THE WINGS.

NOSE

TAIL

WING

How to draw...

WING

DRAW IN THE CONSTRUCTION LINES FOR THE WINGS.

Space Ship One

Draw yours here...

WHEN YOUR DRAWING IS
COMPLETE, REMOVE THE
CONSTRUCTION LINES
WITH AN ERASER.

Splat-a-Fact

SPACE SHIP ONE
MADE THE FIRST
PRIVATELY-FUNDED
SPACE FLIGHT ON 21
JUNE 2004. IT IS
HOPED THAT THIS IS
THE FUTURE OF
SPACE TOURISM.

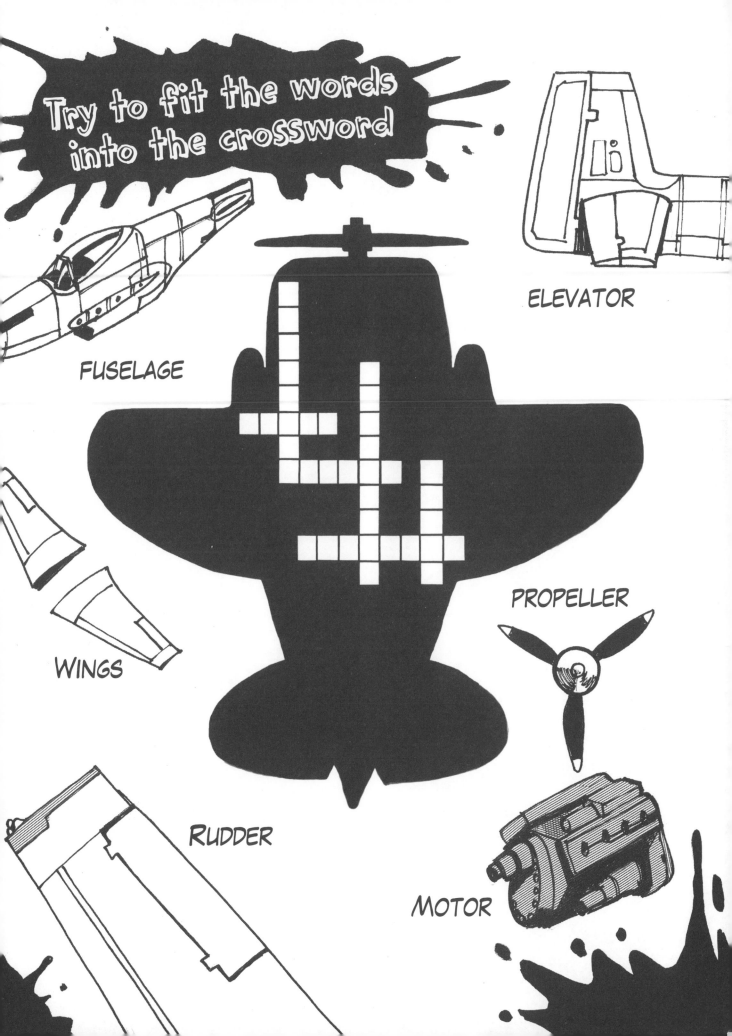

Try to fit the words into the crossword

ELEVATOR

FUSELAGE

WINGS

PROPELLER

RUDDER

MOTOR

SPLAT-a-FACT

IN 1909, THE FIRST AIR SHOW WAS HELD NEAR REIMS IN FRANCE. DURING THE WEEK-LONG EVENT, WHICH ATTRACTED MANY ENTHUSIASTS, AVIATORS FLEW IN COMPETITIONS FOR SPEED AND HEIGHT.

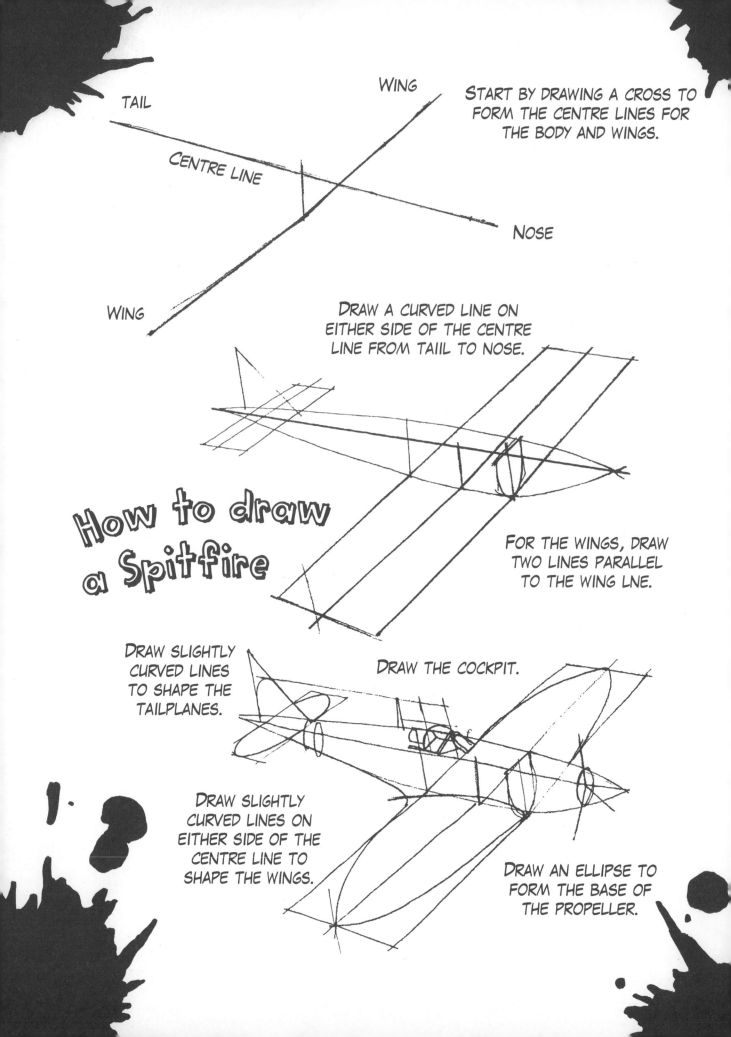

TAIL

WING

CENTRE LINE

NOSE

START BY DRAWING A CROSS TO FORM THE CENTRE LINES FOR THE BODY AND WINGS.

WING

DRAW A CURVED LINE ON EITHER SIDE OF THE CENTRE LINE FROM TAIIL TO NOSE.

How to draw a Spitfire

FOR THE WINGS, DRAW TWO LINES PARALLEL TO THE WING LNE.

DRAW SLIGHTLY CURVED LINES TO SHAPE THE TAILPLANES.

DRAW THE COCKPIT.

DRAW SLIGHTLY CURVED LINES ON EITHER SIDE OF THE CENTRE LINE TO SHAPE THE WINGS.

DRAW AN ELLIPSE TO FORM THE BASE OF THE PROPELLER.

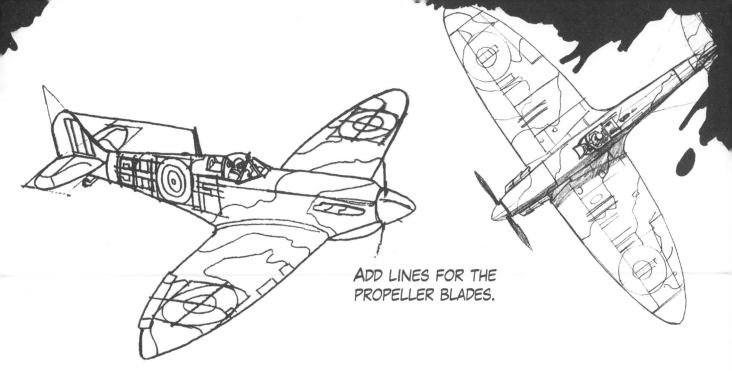

ADD LINES FOR THE
PROPELLER BLADES.

ADD CAMOUFLAGE
AND MARKINGS.

WHEN YOUR DRAWING IS COMPLETE,
REMOVE ANY CONSTRUCTION LINES
WITH AN ERASER.

Draw yours here...

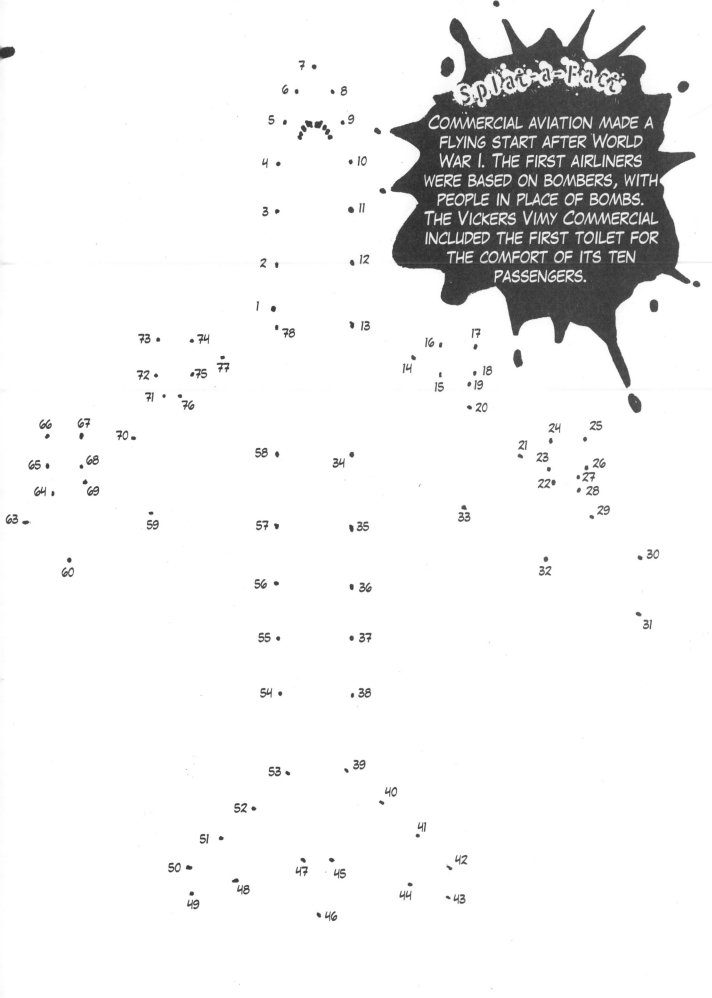

Splat-a-Fact

COMMERCIAL AVIATION MADE A FLYING START AFTER WORLD WAR I. THE FIRST AIRLINERS WERE BASED ON BOMBERS, WITH PEOPLE IN PLACE OF BOMBS. THE VICKERS VIMY COMMERCIAL INCLUDED THE FIRST TOILET FOR THE COMFORT OF ITS TEN PASSENGERS.

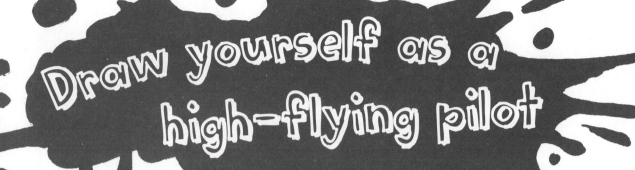

Draw yourself as a high-flying pilot

USE A MIRROR
TO HELP YOU

Colour it in!

Q: What do a flying plane and a pile of dirty washing have in common?

joke!

Fantasy flyers

A: They both don't need hangars!

DRAW YOUR OWN HERE

SPLAT-A-FACT PRIVATE FLYING IS MORE POPULAR TODAY THAN EVER BEFORE. EVEN THOUGH LEARNING TO FLY DEMANDS TIME AND MONEY, THERE ARE MANY AVIATORS WHO DO IT JUST FOR FUN.

Stunt planes

Splat-a-fact

ONE OF THE WORLD'S MOST FAMOUS STUNT PLANES, THE PITTS SPECIAL, WAS DESIGNED IN 1944 IN FLORIDA BY CURTIS PITTS.

Match up the planes with their names!

Low wing   Biplane

Seaplane   Jet

Multi-engine   High wing

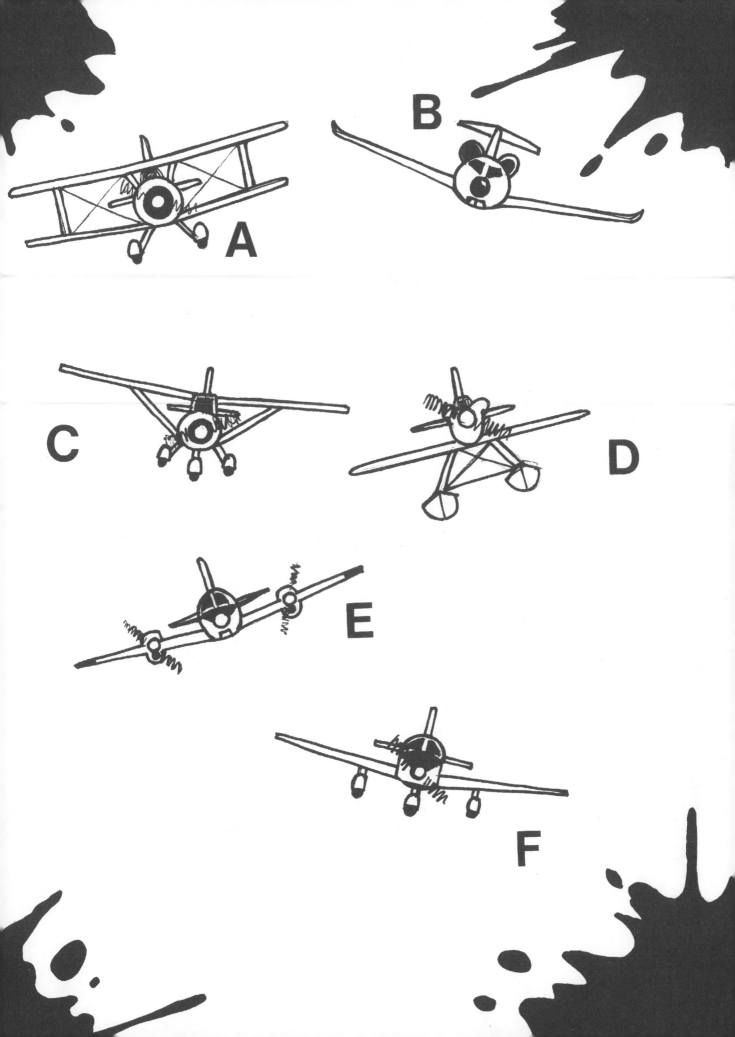

Zooooom

AEROBATICS ARE INCREDIBLE
MANOEUVRES PERFORMED BY A
SKILLED AND SYNCHRONISED FLIGHT
TEAM. THEY HAVE TO BE VERY
CAREFULLY PLANNED.

AEROBATICS ARE PERFORMED
IN AEROPLANES AND GLIDERS
FOR TRAINING, RECREATION,
ENTERTAINMENT AND SPORT.

Finger pilots

Concorde

① ② ③ ④ ⑤ ⑥ ⑦ ⑧ ⑨ ⑩ ⑪ ⑫ ⑬ ⑭ ⑮

AMERICAN AIRWAYS SYSTEM

BOEING 747

ON ⊙ H

U.S. NAVY

21P9

15

Planes picture quiz

A. FIRST MYTHICAL MAN TO FLY
B. FIND TWO SEA PLANES
C. SPOT THE 1930S SPEED RACER
D. FIRST TO CROSS THE CHANNEL
E. FASTEST EVER PLANE
F. WWII HERO OF BATTLE OF BRITAIN
G. AMERICAN WWII BOMBER
H. SPOT TWO MODERN GLIDERS

splat-a-fact

THE TIGER MOTH IS AN IDEAL AEROBATIC MACHINE, DESIGNED BY GEOFFREY DE HAVILLAND IN THE 1930S

Wordsearch 1

PARACHUTE

TAILPLANE

WING

Y	P	W	B	D	Q	E	J	L	S
P	A	R	A	C	H	U	T	E	U
R	E	H	Z	O	F	G	Y	L	I
O	R	P	B	C	C	E	R	T	G
P	Z	A	T	K	R	F	K	T	I
E	O	L	E	P	W	S	D	U	A
L	E	N	G	I	N	E	P	H	K
L	D	F	N	T	P	R	C	S	L
E	M	G	L	I	D	E	R	K	T
R	T	A	I	L	P	L	A	N	E

PROPELLER

ENGINE

GLIDER

SHUTTLE

COCKPIT

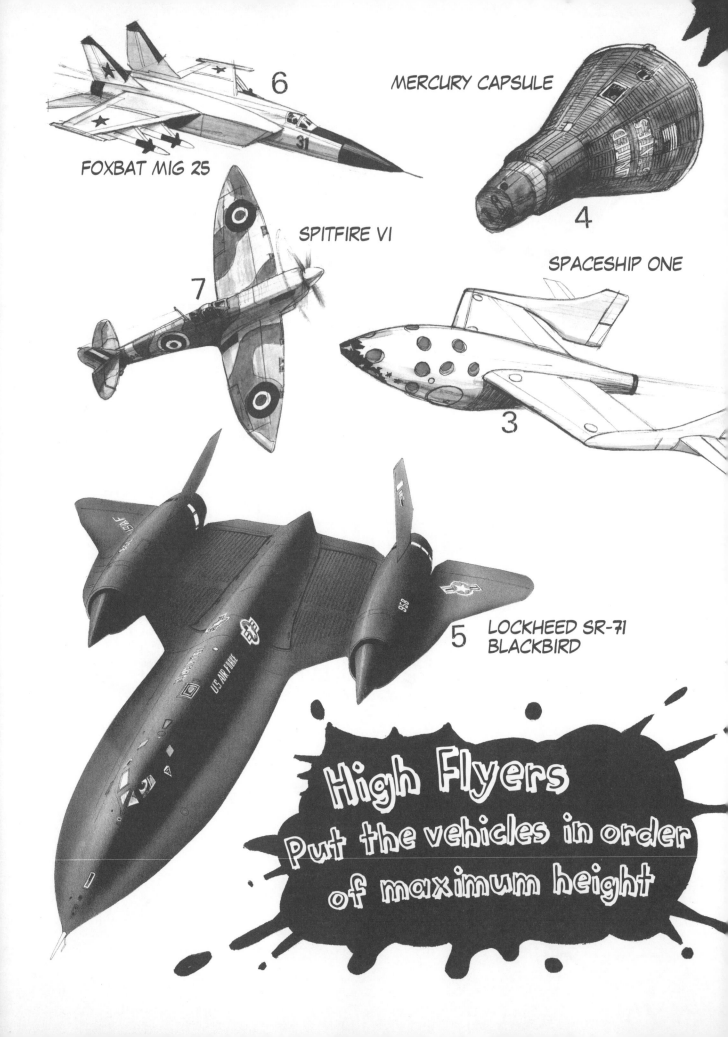

6

MERCURY CAPSULE

FOXBAT MIG 25

4

SPITFIRE VI

SPACESHIP ONE

7

3

LOCKHEED SR-71
BLACKBIRD

5

High Flyers
Put the vehicles in order of maximum height

SOPWITH CAMEL

1

f

g

d

e

MATCH THE
NUMBERED VEHICLES
WITH THE LETTERS
ON THIS PAGE.

A = LOWEST
G = HIGHEST

c

b

2

a

X-15 ROCKET PLANE

Match the planes to the silhouettes

Draw yourself as a pilot

DE HAVILLAND
GIPSY MOTH

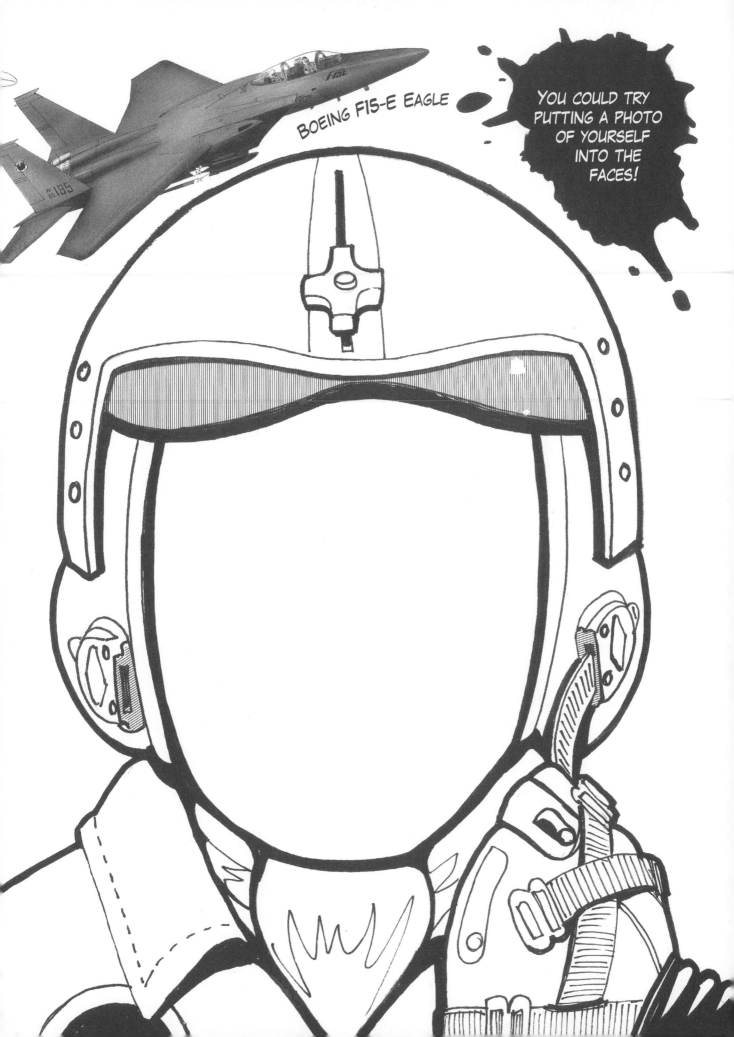

BOEING F15-E EAGLE

YOU COULD TRY PUTTING A PHOTO OF YOURSELF INTO THE FACES!

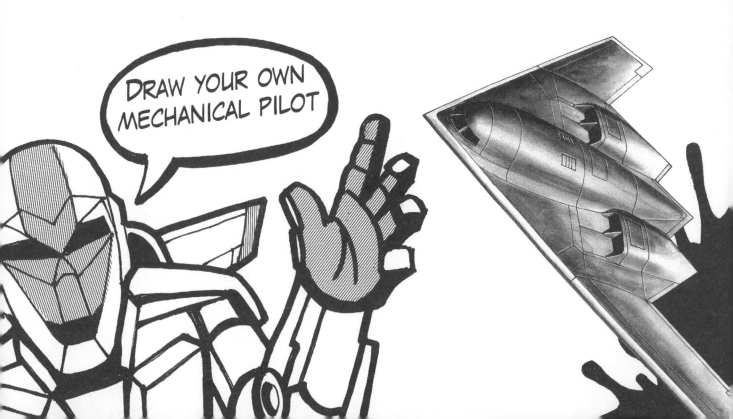

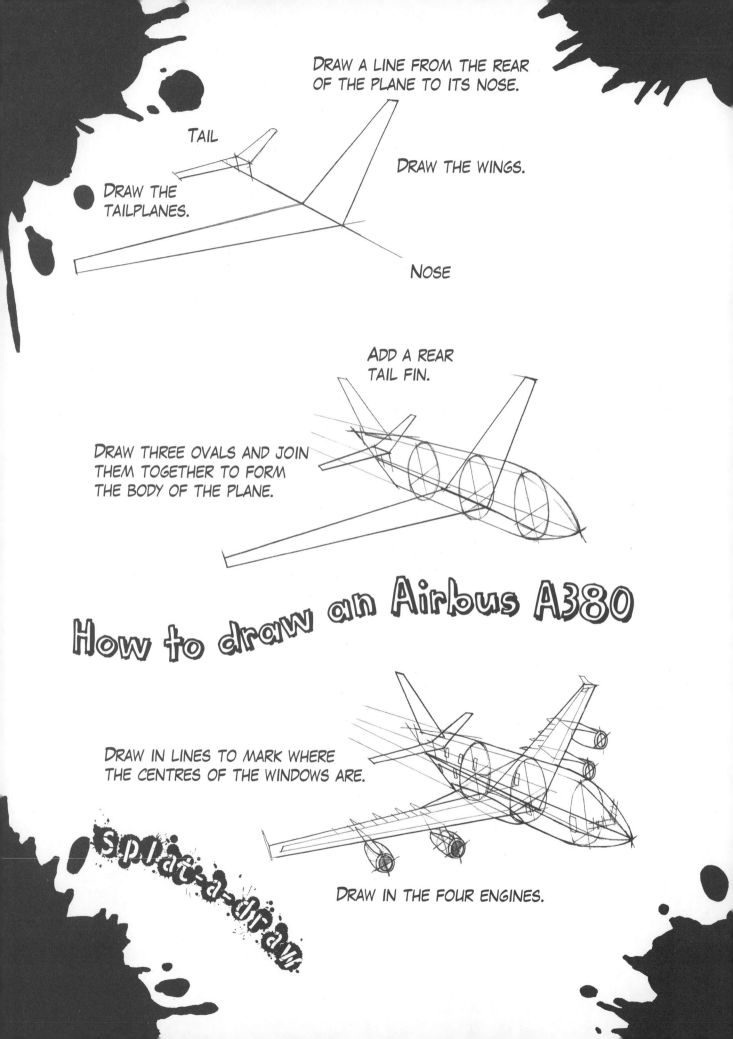

DRAW A LINE FROM THE REAR OF THE PLANE TO ITS NOSE.

TAIL

DRAW THE WINGS.

DRAW THE TAILPLANES.

NOSE

ADD A REAR TAIL FIN.

DRAW THREE OVALS AND JOIN THEM TOGETHER TO FORM THE BODY OF THE PLANE.

How to draw an Airbus A380

DRAW IN LINES TO MARK WHERE THE CENTRES OF THE WINDOWS ARE.

splat-a-draw

DRAW IN THE FOUR ENGINES.

THE 555-SEAT, DOUBLE-DECKER AIRBUS A380 IS THE WORLD'S LARGEST PASSENGER CARRYING AIRLINER. IT HAS BEEN DESIGNED TO CREATE LOWER FUEL EMISSIONS AND LESS NOISE.

DRAW IN THE LOGOS AND WINDOWS. BE CAREFUL TO MAKE THE WINDOWS SMALLER TOWARDS THE TAIL OF THE PLANE.

DRAW YOUR OWN A380 HERE!

splat-a-story

Don't forget to add speech bubbles!

Pack up the plane!

splat-a-fact

THE BOEING 747 JUMBO JET MADE ITS FIRST FLIGHT IN FEBRUARY 1969. IT WAS THE WORLD'S FIRST 'WIDE-BODY' COMMERCIAL AIR TRANSPORT.

Draw your jet here!

splat-a-draw

BIPLANE

JET FIGHTER

Wordsearch 2

BALLOON

PARACHUTE

A	I	R	L	I	N	E	R	S	P
W	B	Y	K	U	E	D	R	H	A
F	V	I	T	S	L	L	E	T	R
H	O	R	P	F	C	Y	U	R	A
E	A	F	G	L	I	D	E	R	C
V	R	H	S	E	A	U	I	L	H
O	L	P	G	N	J	N	B	M	U
S	E	A	P	L	A	N	E	X	T
T	M	B	A	L	L	O	O	N	E
J	E	T	F	I	G	H	T	E	R

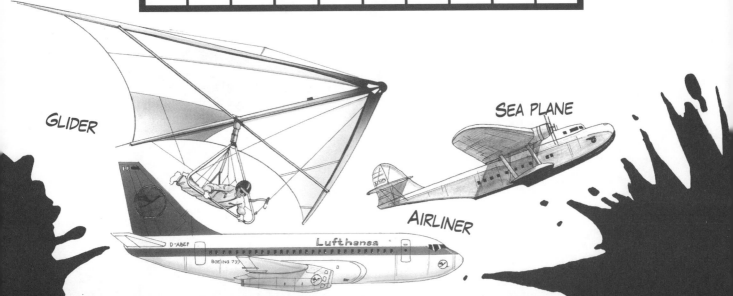

GLIDER

SEA PLANE

AIRLINER

A: A jumbo jet!

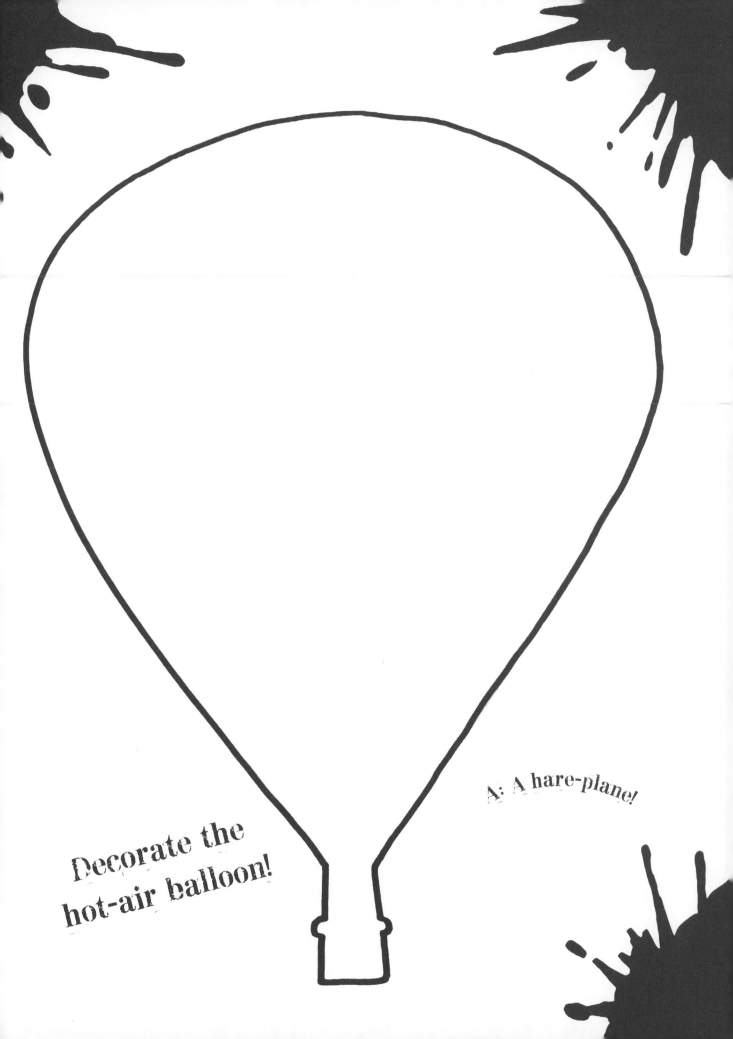

Decorate the hot-air balloon!

A: A hare-plane!

Give each character a name

Can you complete the other half of the jet?

Splat-a-Fact

THE HARRIER 'JUMP JET' CAN TAKE OFF VERTICALLY AND HOVER LIKE A HELICOPTER BY DIRECTING ITS JET'S FOUR NOZZLES DOWNWARD.

Splat-a-Fact

THE FOUR SPACE
SHUTTLES - ATLANTIS,
COLUMBIA, DISCOVERY
AND ENDEAVOUR - DEPLOY
AND RECOVER
SATELLITES, CARRY
SCIENTIFIC EXPERIMENTS
INTO SPACE, AND CARRY
OUT TOP-SECRET
MILITARY MISSIONS.

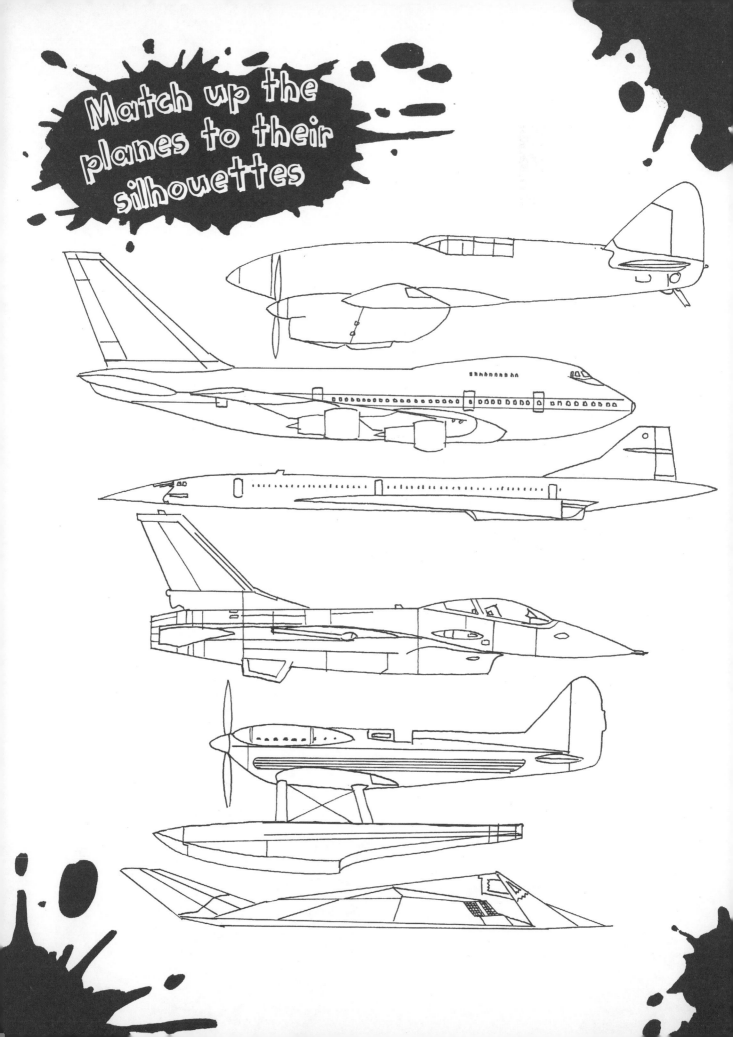

Match up the planes to their silhouettes

splat-a-match

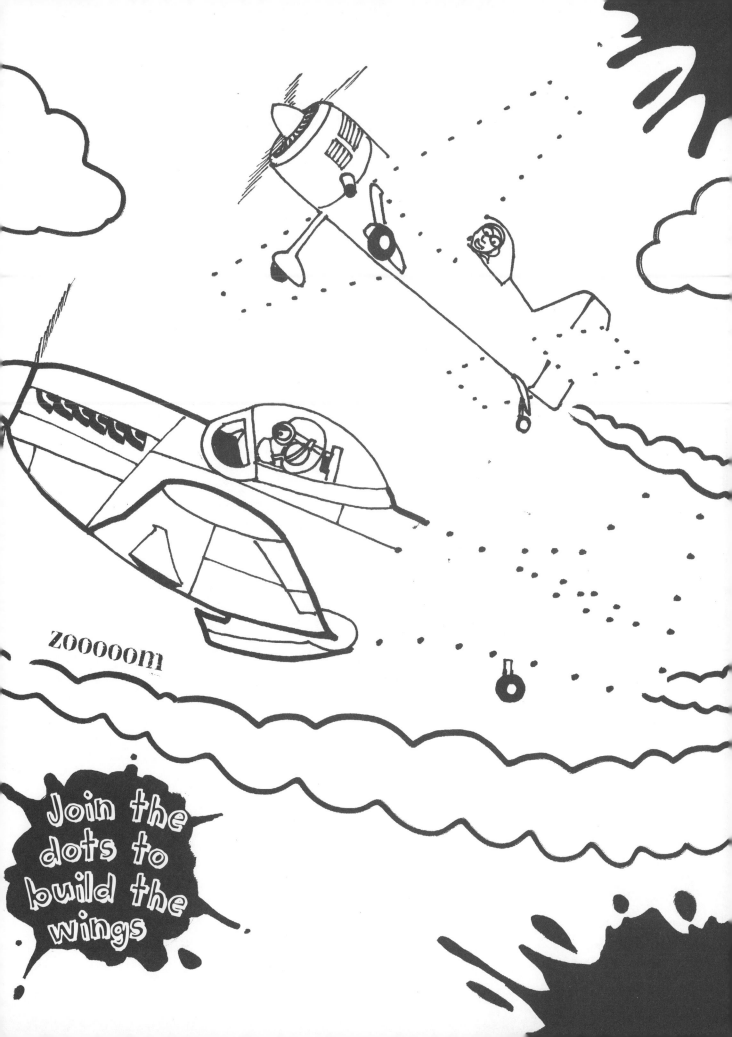

zooooom!

Join the dots to build the wings

Can you fly the plane to the airport?

HYDRANT REFUELLER

viva*

CATERING TRUCK

AIRCRAFT TUG

EERO SAARINEN'S TERMINAL

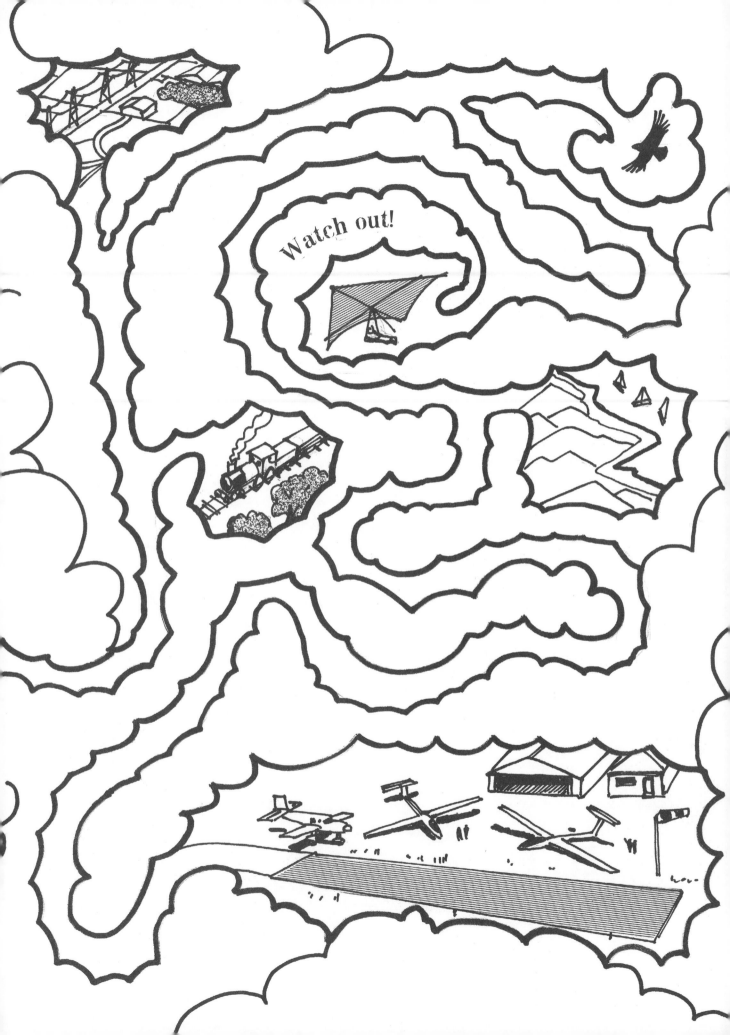

Spot the difference 2

joke!

Q: What flies and serves sandwiches?

How to draw Concorde

REAR

DRAW A LINE FROM THE
NOSE OF CONCORDE TO
ITS REAR.

NOSE

SKETCH A LARGE TRIANGLE
FOR THE WINGS

WINGS

DRAW THE POSITION
OF THE TAIL FIN

SKETCH IN THE BODY AND
THE LONG POINTED NOSE
OF CONCORDE.

ADD DETAIL TO
THE SHAPES

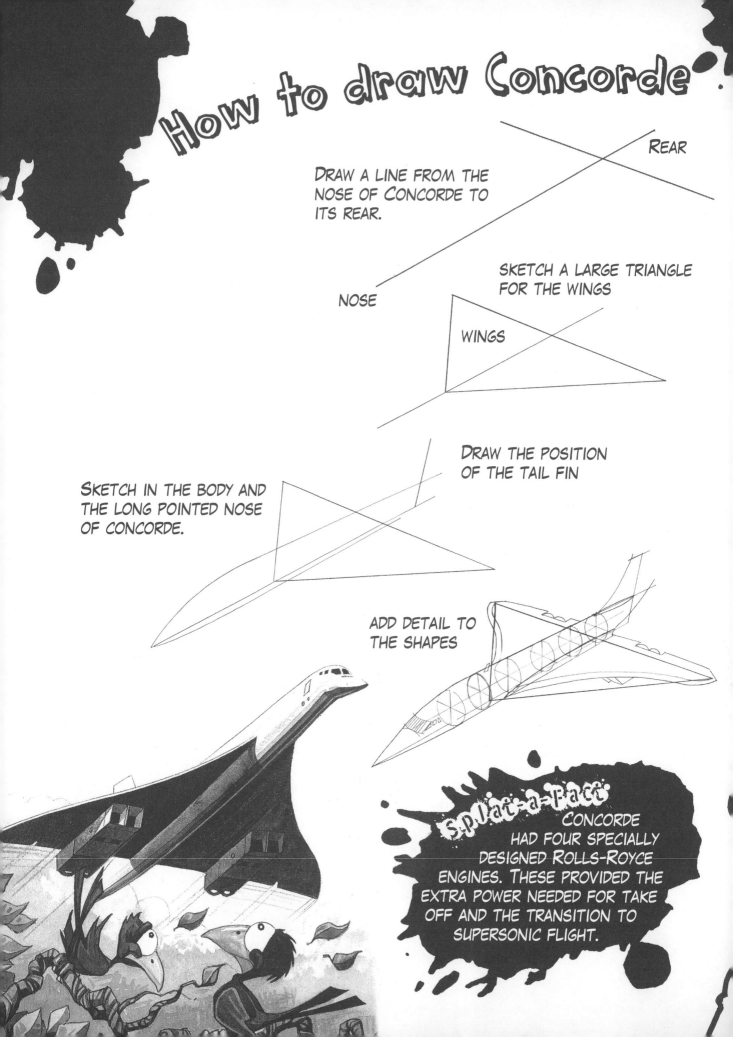

Splat-a-Fact

CONCORDE
HAD FOUR SPECIALLY
DESIGNED ROLLS-ROYCE
ENGINES. THESE PROVIDED THE
EXTRA POWER NEEDED FOR TAKE
OFF AND THE TRANSITION TO
SUPERSONIC FLIGHT.

LIGHTLY SHADE IN AREAS
OF SHADOW ON THE MAIN
BODY AND WINGS

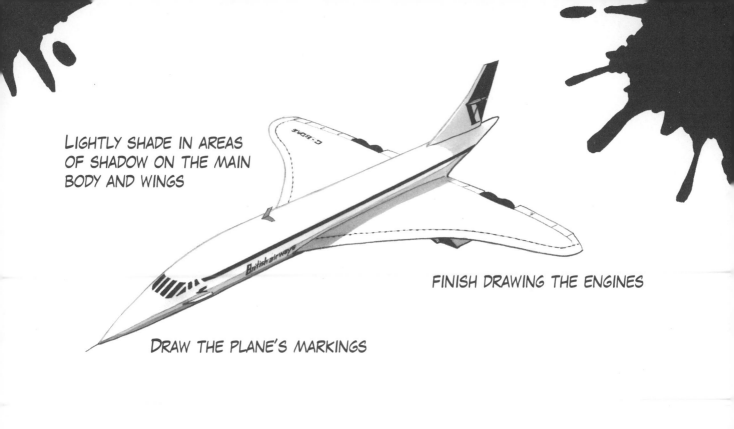

FINISH DRAWING THE ENGINES

DRAW THE PLANE'S MARKINGS

DRAW YOURS
HERE!

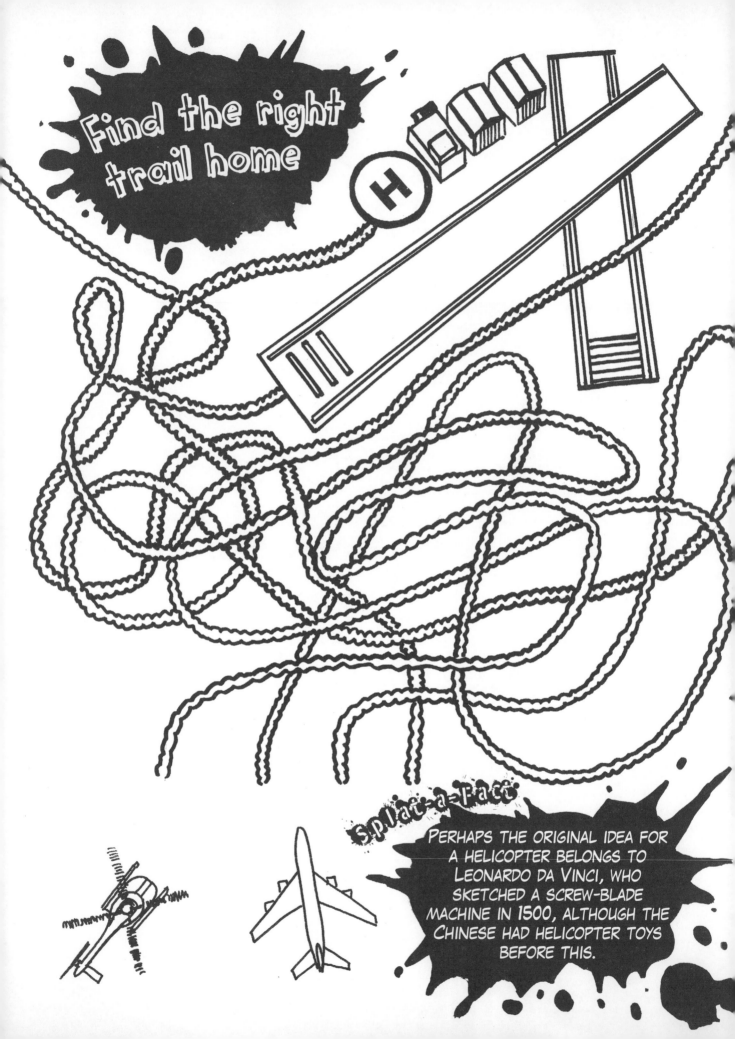

Find the right trail home

Splat-a-Fact

PERHAPS THE ORIGINAL IDEA FOR A HELICOPTER BELONGS TO LEONARDO DA VINCI, WHO SKETCHED A SCREW-BLADE MACHINE IN 1500, ALTHOUGH THE CHINESE HAD HELICOPTER TOYS BEFORE THIS.

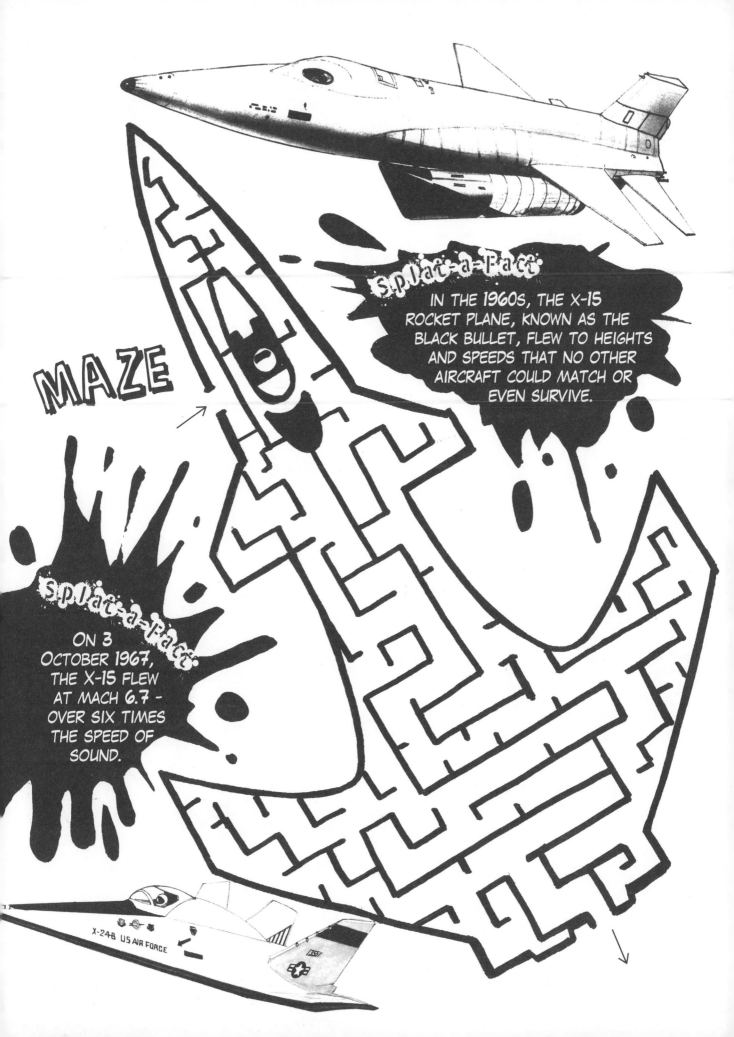

MAZE

Splat-a-Fact
IN THE 1960s, THE X-15 ROCKET PLANE, KNOWN AS THE BLACK BULLET, FLEW TO HEIGHTS AND SPEEDS THAT NO OTHER AIRCRAFT COULD MATCH OR EVEN SURVIVE.

Splat-a-Fact
ON 3 OCTOBER 1967, THE X-15 FLEW AT MACH 6.7 - OVER SIX TIMES THE SPEED OF SOUND.

X-24B US AIR FORCE

Find 9 display aircraft like this: ✈

Write about what is going on in these pictures

Airport crossword puzzle

TERMINAL

RUNWAY

WINDSOCK

TOWER

HANGAR

RADAR

ANSWERS

MATCH THE AIRCRAFT PARTS WITH THE AIRCRAFT

HOW MANY BALLOONS ARE THERE?

FIFTY

FLYDOKU 1

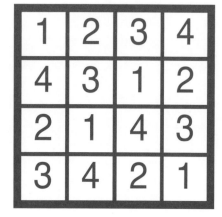

PLANE CROSSWORD

ELEVATOR
MOTOR
PROPELLER
RUDDER WINGS
FUSELAGE

WHERE WOULD THESE AIRCRAFT LAND?

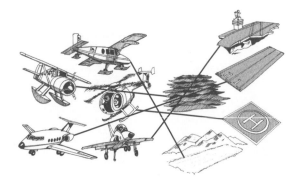

JOIN THE DOTS

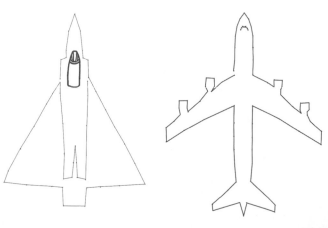

HOW MANY AIRCRAFT ARE THERE? EIGHT

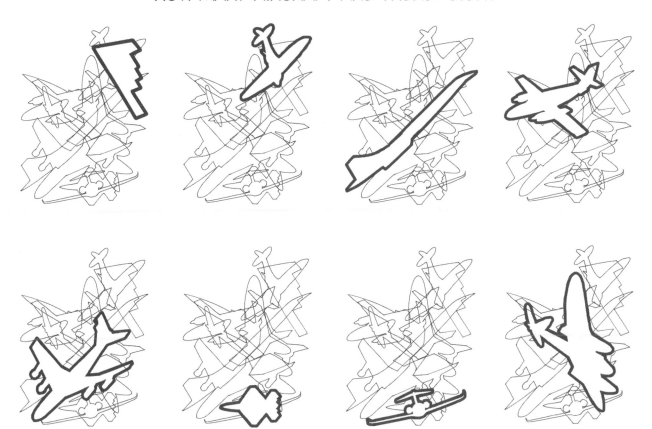

MATCH UP THE PLANES WITH THEIR NAMES

A = BIPLANE
B = JET
C = HIGH WING
D = SEAPLANE
E = MULTI ENGINE
F = LOW WING

PLANES PICTURE QUIZ

A = 3
B = 2 & 10
C = 6
D = 9
E = 4
F = 8
G = 13
H = 1 & 11

WORDSEARCH 1

Y	P	W	B	D	Q	E	J	L	S
P	A	R	A	C	H	U	T	E	U
R	E	H	Z	O	F	G	Y	L	I
O	R	P	B	C	C	E	R	T	G
P	Z	A	T	K	R	F	K	T	I
E	O	L	E	P	W	S	D	U	A
L	E	N	G	I	N	E	P	H	K
L	D	F	N	T	P	R	C	S	L
E	M	G	L	I	D	E	R	K	T
R	T	A	I	L	P	L	A	N	E

A=1   E=3
B=7   F=2
C=5   G=4
D=6

MATCH THE PLANES TO THE SILHOUETTES

MATCH THE PLANE PARTS TO THE CONTAINERS

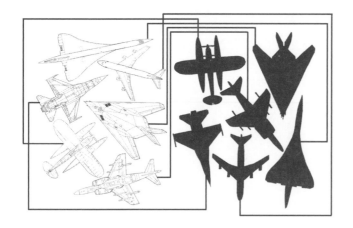

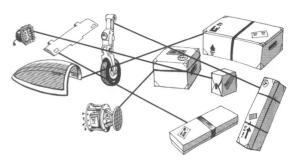

FLYDOKU 2

1	3	2	4
4	2	3	1
3	1	4	2
2	4	1	3

WORDSEARCH 2

A	I	R	L	I	N	E	R	S	P
W	B	Y	K	U	E	D	R	H	A
F	V	I	T	S	L	L	E	T	R
H	O	R	P	F	C	Y	U	R	A
E	A	F	G	L	I	D	E	R	C
V	R	H	S	E	A	U	I	L	H
O	L	P	G	N	J	N	B	M	U
S	E	A	P	L	A	N	E	X	T
T	M	B	A	L	L	O	O	N	E
J	E	T	F	I	G	H	T	E	R

HELP THE PILOTS FIND THEIR AIRCRAFT

MATCH THE PLANES TO THE SILHOUETTES

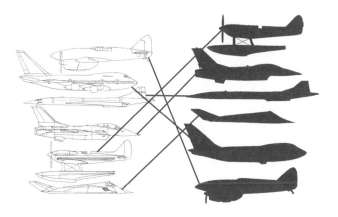

SPOT THE DIFFERENCE 1

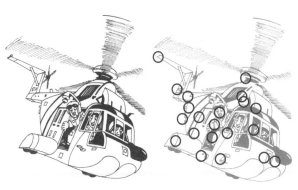

FLY THE PLANE TO THE AIRPORT

FIND THE AIRFIELD THROUGH THE CLOUDS

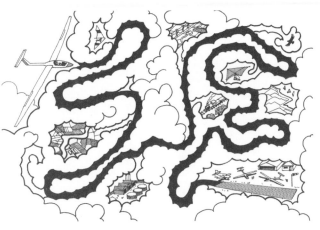

HOW MANY HELICOPTERS ARE THERE?

TWENTY-FIVE

CRACK THE CODE

BEHIND   THE   HANGAR

SPOT THE DIFFERENCE 2

FIND THE RIGHT TRAIL HOME

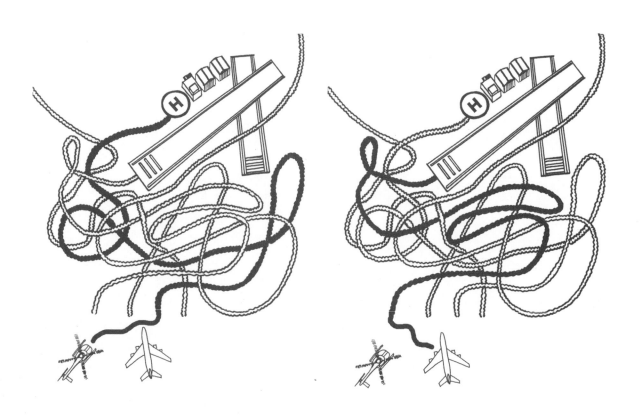